NATIONAL GEOGRAPHIC KiDS

weird but true!

ANIMALS

**300** outrageous
facts about
wacky wildlife

D0029877

THAT'S WEIRD!

GIRAFFES WERE ONCE CALLED CAMEL-LEOPARDS.

NATIONAL
GEOGRAPHIC
KiDS

weird but true!

ANIMALS

300 outrageous facts about wacky wildlife

NATIONAL GEOGRAPHIC
WASHINGTON, D.C.

After a chase, a **cheetah** has to wait about **30 minutes** to catch its breath before it can **eat.**

CHEETAHS CAN **CHIRP.**

SOME **FEMALE KATYDIDS** IN **BORNEO LOOK** **LIKE PINK LEAVES.**

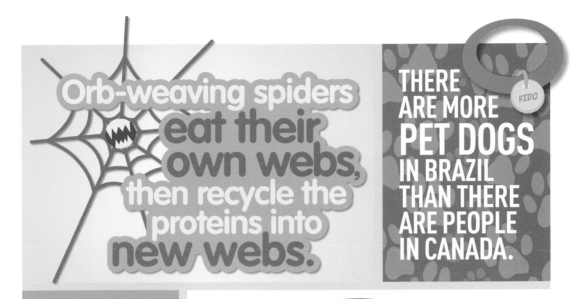

Orb-weaving spiders **eat their own webs,** then recycle the proteins into **new webs.**

THERE ARE MORE **PET DOGS** IN BRAZIL THAN THERE ARE PEOPLE IN CANADA.

FIDO

An **insect** called a **midge** beats its **wings** more than **62,000** times a minute.

The expression **to shed** crocodile tears (or to express fake emotion) exists in at least 50 different languages.

The smalleye pygmy shark

can fit in your hand.

GOLDFISH CAN GROW TO THE SIZE OF A TWO-LITER SODA BOTTLE.

**Black rhino horns** have grown to be **5 feet long.** (1.5 m) That's probably **taller** than most **kids.**

A HONEY BADGER'S POWERFUL **JAWS** AND **SHARP TEETH** CAN CRUSH A TORTOISE'S SHELL.

**A HONEY BADGER'S SKIN** IS SO THICK THAT THE ANIMAL IS UNHARMED BY **BEE STINGS AND PORCUPINE QUILLS.**

THE DUTCH NATIONAL POLICE HAVE TRAINED A BALD EAGLE TO TAKE DOWN SMALL DRONES.

VENOM from the BRAZILIAN PIT VIPER WAS USED TO CREATE A DRUG TO TREAT HIGH BLOOD PRESSURE.

THERE ARE ABOUT 20 HAMSTER BREEDS.

Scientists think that *Tyrannosaurus rex* could run at a speed of only about **5 miles** an hour. (8 km/h)

13

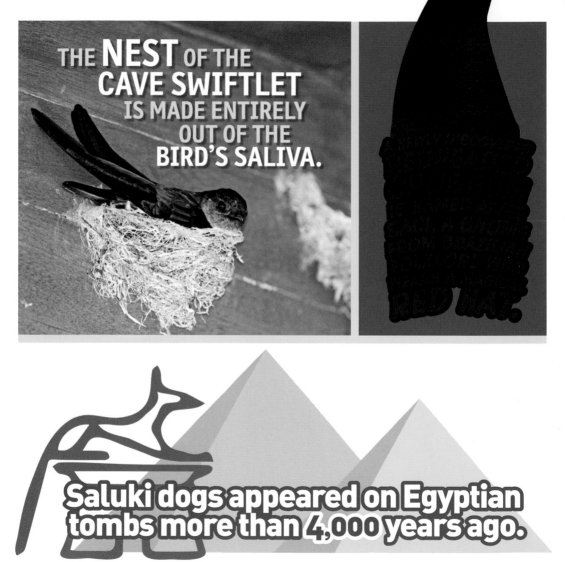

THE **NEST** OF THE **CAVE SWIFTLET** IS MADE ENTIRELY OUT OF THE **BIRD'S SALIVA.**

**Saluki dogs appeared on Egyptian tombs more than 4,000 years ago.**

Scientists have **trained** **archerfish** to recognize different **human faces.**

**VIETNAMESE MOSSY FROG TADPOLES SOMETIMES RIDE ON AIR BUBBLES.**

The South American **potoo bird** has slits in its eyelids—allowing it to detect movement without opening its eyes.

# A great white shark's liver makes up a quarter of its body weight.

MMM, LIVER.

**Gila monsters** use their **bladder** to **store water.**

SOME OF THE FIRST ANIMALS TO RETURN TO MOUNT ST. HELENS AFTER ITS 1980 ERUPTION **WERE BEETLES AND SPIDERS.**

**Snails sometimes travel** in the slime trails **of other snails to save energy.**

SOMETIMES, **ELF OWLS PLAY DEAD.**

A group of **sheepdogs** on Middle Island, Australia, is trained to **protect a penguin colony** from foxes.

Polar bear paws can be as wide as a dinner plate.

In England, finding a spider in your wedding dress is considered good luck.

20

**Brittle stars** have **special lenses** that let them use their **shells to see.**

AN
**ARMORED PANGOLIN**
CAN ROLL INTO A BALL
SO TOUGH THAT A LION
CAN'T BITE THROUGH IT.

The dinosaur *Therizinosaurus* had claws as long as a skateboard that it likely used to grab plants.

There are more pet birds in Europe than there are people in California, U.S.A.

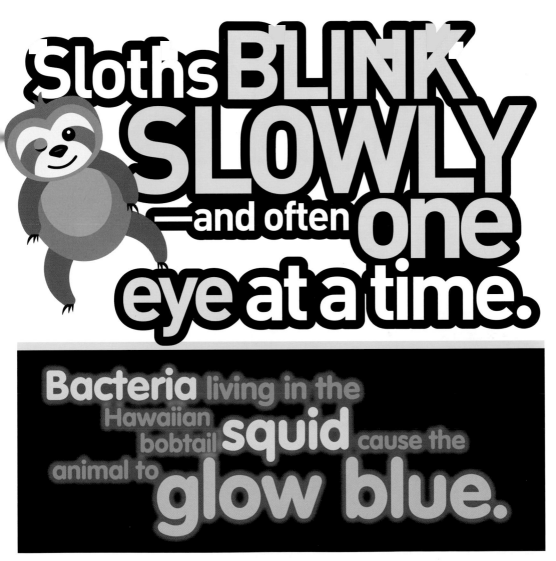

Sloths **BLINK SLOWLY**—and often **one eye at a time.**

**Bacteria** living in the Hawaiian bobtail **squid** cause the animal to **glow blue.**

LABRADOR RETRIEVERS HAVE A **TAPERED TAIL** THAT **HELPS THEM STEER IN WATER.**

Some **20 million** Mexican free-tailed **bats** live in a cave in Texas, U.S.A. That's more than the population of Chile.

BATS CAN **EAT** UP TO **1,200** MOSQUITOES IN AN HOUR.

SOME
**MONKEYS**
USE COCONUT
FIBERS, TWIGS, OR EVEN
HAIR TO **FLOSS.**

Sea turtles **eat** box jellyfish, one of the most **venomous creatures** in the world.

IN JAPAN, TUNNELS WERE CREATED TO HELP TURTLES SAFELY CROSS TRAIN TRACKS.

# Scorpions glow at night if you shine a black light on them.

**MILLIONS** of sardines swim together in dense, glistening "balls" to evade predators.

# A GROUP OF CATS IS CALLED A CLOWDER.

**MOUNTAIN GOATS** AREN'T GOATS; THEY ARE IN THE **ANTELOPE** FAMILY.

THE SOUTHERN GRASSHOPPER **MOUSE STANDS** ON ITS HIND LEGS AND **HOWLS** TO CLAIM ITS TERRITORY.

Baby Suriname toads are born from holes in their mom's back.

**Orangutans** sometimes use bundles of **leaves** as umbrellas when it **rains.**

Crows play pranks on each other.

A Peruvian rain forest caterpillar disguised as a leaf has four tentacles on its back that pop out when it is disturbed by sound.

The **bird-dung crab spider** looks and smells like **bird poop** to **lure** insects.

A **flounder's eye** migrates from **one side of its body** to the other as it ages.

**Baby camels** don't have a hump.

PENGUINS ARE THE ONLY BIRDS THAT CAN'T FOLD THEIR WINGS.

A SPECIES OF **TIGER MOTH** MAKES **CLICKING SOUNDS** THAT JAM BATS' SONAR.

The largest known **oyster,** found off the coast **of Denmark,** is the size of a **large shoe.**

Brazilian free-tailed bats **can fly faster** than a car driving on a highway.

The
slow loris produces
venom on
the inside
of its
elbows.

RESEARCHERS FOUND THAT SEVERAL FISH SPECIES USE URINE TO COMMUNICATE.

GIANT TORTOISES SOAK IN POOLS OF WATER IN A VOLCANO CRATER ON THE GALÁPAGOS ISLANDS.

ELEPHANTS HAVE BEEN FITTED WITH PROSTHETIC LIMBS.

**Elephants** will roll in the **dust** or **mud** to protect themselves from **sunburn.**

The smallest bird egg is about the size of a pea.

Baby **echidnas** *resemble the* **Niffler** *from Fantastic Beasts and Where to Find Them.*

Snails can regrow their eyes.

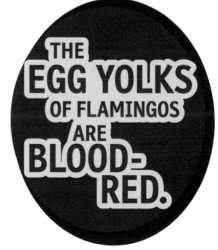

THE EGG YOLKS OF FLAMINGOS ARE BLOOD-RED.

**Puss caterpillars** can cause "stings" more painful than a bee's.

A JAPANESE ENGINEER
STUDIED **OWL FLIGHT**
TO HELP MAKE THE SHINKANSEN
**BULLET TRAINS**
QUIETER AS THEY REACH
SPEEDS OF
**185 MILES** AN HOUR.
(300 km/h)

# THERE ARE MORE KANGAROOS

# THAN PEOPLE IN AUSTRALIA.

A 6.5-FOOT (2-m) **KANGAROO** SPECIES THAT LIVED IN **AUSTRALIA** 40,000 YEARS AGO COULDN'T **HOP.**

Birds known as **brown thrashers** can sing more than **1,000 songs.**

**A DRAGONFLY'S EYES TAKE UP MOST OF ITS HEAD.**

**POLAR BEARS** HAVE **BLACK SKIN.**

A **blue dragon sea slug** can steal a Portuguese man-of-war's stinging cells and release their **venom** when threatened by a predator.

YOUNG **LOBSTERS** SOMETIMES HITCH A RIDE ON **JELLYFISH** TO SAVE ENERGY— EATING THE JELLYFISH AS THEY GO!

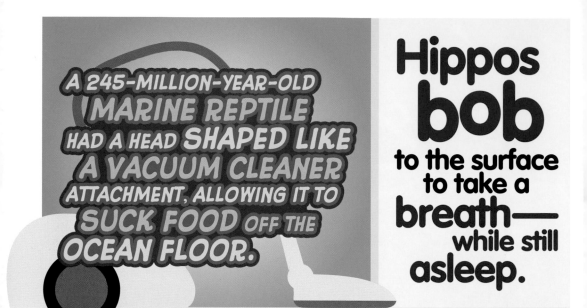

A 245-MILLION-YEAR-OLD **MARINE REPTILE** HAD A HEAD **SHAPED LIKE A VACUUM CLEANER** ATTACHMENT, ALLOWING IT TO **SUCK FOOD** OFF THE OCEAN FLOOR.

# Hippos **bob**
to the surface to take a **breath—** while still **asleep.**

The **chocolate chip**
# sea star
got its name from the dark brown horns that cover its body for protection.

A PLATYPUS'S BILL CAN SENSE ELECTRIC CURRENTS.

Dogs can be trained to sniff out some cancers in humans.

**A RING-TAILED LEMUR HAS EXACTLY 13 BLACK AND 13 WHITE RINGS ON ITS TAIL.**

Some people become **allergic** **to red meat** after being **bitten** by a lone star **tick.**

NAKED MOLE RATS CAN

**MATAMATA TURTLES**
CREATE A VACUUM IN THEIR MOUTHS

TO SUCK UP PREY AND SWALLOW

IT WHOLE.

To protect themselves from the sun, some types of sea urchins cover up with algae and bits of coral.

MOVE THEIR FRONT TEETH SEPARATELY— LIKE CHOPSTICKS.

A **candymaker** in the early 1900s claimed that he named the **lollipop** after a famous racehorse called **Lolly Pop.**

Because bats are considered **lucky** in **China**, the Chinese word for **"bat"** sounds the same as the word for **"good fortune."**

There are
more than
5,000
different
species of
ladybugs.

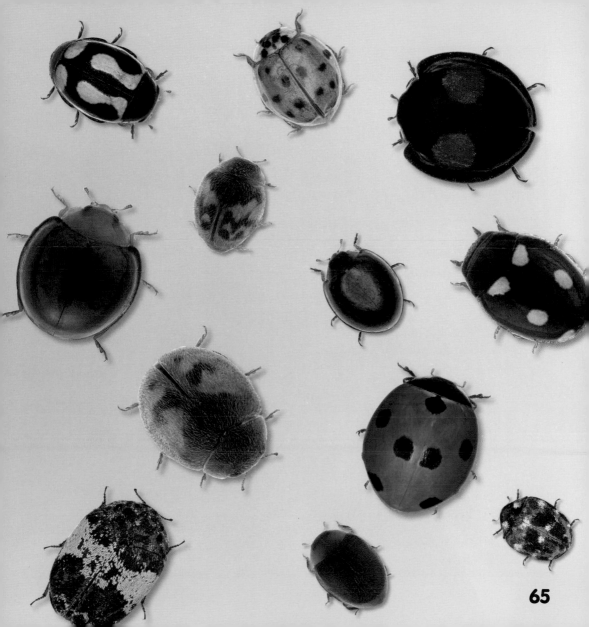

A BEAVER WALKED INTO A MARYLAND, U.S.A., STORE AND LOOKED AT SOME ARTIFICIAL CHRISTMAS TREES BEFORE WILDLIFE OFFICIALS RESCUED IT.

THE CALL OF RED-EYED TREE FROGS SOUNDS LIKE A BABY RATTLE.

The poisonous **toxin** of the geographic **cone snail** is powerful enough to **kill a human.**

A COLLECTOR ONCE BOUGHT A DODO BIRD SKELETON FOR MORE THAN $430,000.

TO PREVENT **SEA TURTLES** FROM **GETTING CAUGHT** IN **FISHING NETS,** RESEARCHERS ARE DEVELOPING **NETS** WITH **GREEN LED LIGHTS** ATTACHED THAT KEEP THE TURTLES AWAY.

# TO RAISE AWARENESS ABOUT POLLUTION, A PORTUGUESE ARTIST CREATES ANIMAL SCULPTURES OUT OF TRASH.

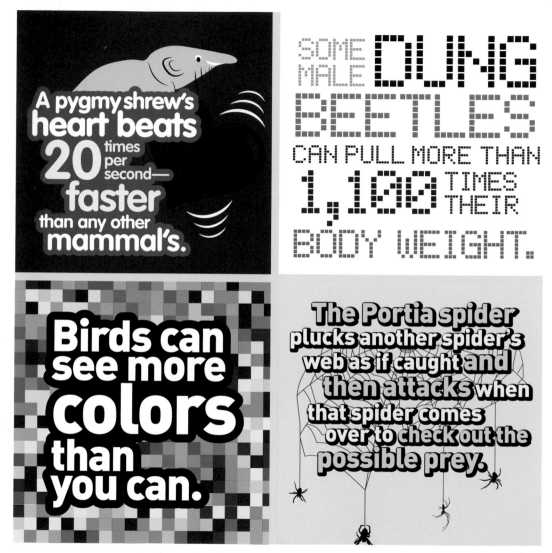

A pygmy shrew's **heart beats** **20** times per second— **faster** than any other **mammal's.**

SOME MALE **DUNG BEETLES** CAN PULL MORE THAN **1,100** TIMES THEIR BODY WEIGHT.

**Birds can see more colors than you can.**

The Portia spider plucks another spider's web as if caught and then attacks when that spider comes over to check out the possible prey.

After catching a fish, an **osprey** carries its **prey headfirst** to ease wind resistance as it flies.

**OSPREYS** WILL FLY AS MANY AS **160,000 MILES** DURING THEIR (257,500 km) **20-YEAR** LIFE SPAN.

WEST AFRICAN **LUNGFISH** CAN SURVIVE YEARS ON LAND BY **WRAPPING THEMSELVES** UP IN A MUCUS COCOON AND **BURROWING** IN THE **MUD.**

**THE PYGMY SHREW NEEDS TO EAT ABOUT EVERY HOUR OR IT WILL DIE.**

SOME **FROG SALIVA** IS THICKER THAN **HONEY.**

**Worms** live in the arms of the bat star, a type of **sea star.**

FOREST ANTELOPES CALLED **DUIKERS** USE SECRETIONS FROM GLANDS BELOW THEIR EYES TO **MARK THEIR TERRITORY.**

When food is running low, **marine iguanas** can shrink, then grow back to their full length when food is abundant.

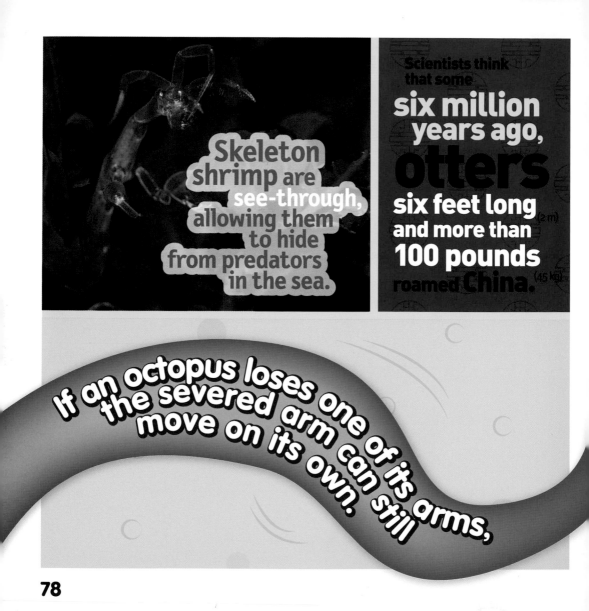

**Skeleton shrimp are see-through, allowing them to hide from predators in the sea.**

Scientists think that some **six million years ago,** **otters** **six feet long** (2 m) **and more than 100 pounds** (45 kg) roamed **China.**

If an octopus loses one of its arms, the severed arm can still move on its own.

THE UNITED ARAB EMIRATES

MR. FALCON
BIRD OF PREY
M

01.01.1981
30.03.2009
20.03.2019

THE
**UNITED ARAB EMIRATES**
ISSUES PASSPORTS **FOR FALCONS,**
the country's **NATIONAL BIRD.**

A **HOSPITAL** IN THE UNITED ARAB EMIRATES
**TREATS**
**ONLY FALCONS.**

79

# THE LOOSE FLAP OF SKIN UNDERNEATH A LIZARD'S NECK IS CALLED A DEWLAP.

GRAY SEALS SEE BETTER UNDERWATER THAN ABOVE THE SURFACE.

The venomous **bull ant** of Australia uses its **jaws** to hold on as it repeatedly stings its victim.

Some **bumblebees** can learn to pull a string in order to get a treat.

PINK DOLPHINS GET PINKER WHEN EXCITED OR SURPRISED, SIMILAR TO BLUSHING IN HUMANS.

# Baby puffins are called pufflings.

THE WORD "UKULELE" TRANSLATES AS "JUMPING FLEA" —FROM THE WAY A MUSICIAN'S FINGERS JUMP ACROSS THE INSTRUMENT.

A newly discovered species of **frog** glows **blue-green** under **ultraviolet light.**

**Footprints** of a long-necked **sauropod,** found in Australia, are as long as **two skateboards.**

85

There is a species of **jellyfish** that looks like a **fried egg.**

A **unicornfish** gets its **name** from the **LONG HORN** on its **FOREHEAD.**

THE WORLD'S LARGEST **INSECT** IS SIX TIMES LONGER THAN THE WORLD'S SMALLEST BIRD.

A zoo in Sydney, Australia, lets its **big cats** sniff scents from spices and **28 different essential oils** to keep them active and engaged.

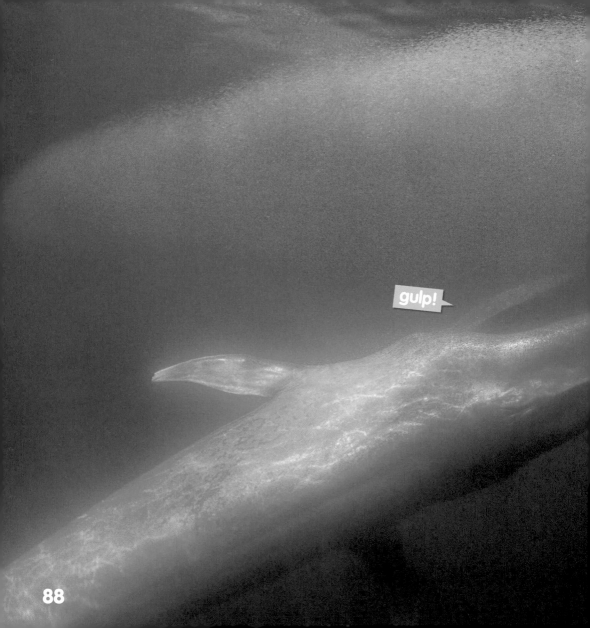

Blue whales catch **500,000 calories of food** in one mouthful—that's the equivalent of **1,000 cheeseburgers!**

# PIGS CAN BE TAUGHT TO PLAY A SIMPLE VIDEO GAME.

A GROUP OF **DUCKS** LIVE ON THE **ROOF** OF THE PEABODY HOTEL IN MEMPHIS, TENNESSEE, U.S.A., IN THEIR OWN BUILDING WORTH $200,000.

**MICE** STARTED LIVING IN HUMAN SETTLEMENTS 15,000 YEARS AGO.

DESERT TORTOISES DIG HOLES IN THE DIRT TO COLLECT RAINWATER.

A fin that runs from an electric eel's head to the tip of its tail helps it swim backward with ease.

An **Australian sheep**
long overdue for a **shear** had enough

**WOOL**

to make 30 sweaters.

**SCIENTISTS' TEST BEES'**

**HONEY**

NEAR AN AIRPORT IN GERMANY

**TO DETECT POLLUTANTS** IN THE **ENVIRONMENT.**

A study found that **Atlas day geckos** living at HIGH altitudes **cuddle to stay warm.**

The northern snakehead **fish** can survive **four days out of water** if kept moist.

**Hyenas** roamed what is now **North America 1.5 million** years ago.

# Young chimpanzees play-wrestle, just like human kids.

A HANDFUL OF GARDEN SOIL CAN CONTAIN THOUSANDS OF ROUNDWORMS.

Desert-dwelling dorcas gazelles don't urinate.

The first **Siamese cat** to come to the United States was given as a **gift to President Rutherford B. Hayes.**

# RESEARCHERS HAVE DEVELOPED A FLU VACCINE FOR DOGS.

eek!

AMERICAN CROWS ................................... FIVE YEARS OR LONGER.

IF A TINY INSECT CALLED A **mite** WERE THE SIZE OF A **human,** IT WOULD MOVE AT SPEEDS OF **1,300 miles** (2,092 km/h) AN HOUR.

**ANT SPECIES** LIVING IN **CENTRAL** AND **SOUTH AMERICA CAN SWIM THREE TIMES FASTER** THAN AN OLYMPIC SWIMMER, **RELATIVE** TO THEIR SIZE.

A **GIANT** ANTEATER'S SENSE OF SMELL IS **40 TIMES STRONGER** THAN YOURS.

# A GIANT ANTEATER'S TONGUE IS MORE THAN TWO FEET LONG. (0.6 m)

MARSH RABBITS CAN SWIM AND DIVE UNDERWATER.

HARRY POTTER + SEVERUS SNAPE

# Harryplax severus:
## a new species of crab that lives off the coast of Guam

YOU CAN **EXPLORE JAPAN'S ONOMICHI CITY**, KNOWN FOR ITS LARGE CAT POPULATION, IN AN ONLINE STREET MAP DESIGNED FROM A **CAT'S POINT OF VIEW.**

*ELEPHANTS AVOID EATING* **LEAVES** *WITH* **ANTS** *ON THEM BECAUSE* **ANTS IRRITATE** *THEIR* **TRUNK.**

Small **birds** known as Clark's nutcrackers can **store** some **100,000** seeds for the **winter.**

# THE LEAF DEER GOT ITS NAME BECAUSE THE ANIMAL IS SO SMALL THAT IT CAN BE WRAPPED UP IN A LARGE LEAF.

**Cuttlefish** have **W-shaped pupils** in bright light.

THE **BIRD** INSIDE THE WORLD'S BIGGEST CUCKOO CLOCK, LOCATED IN GERMANY, IS MORE THAN **14 FEET LONG AND WEIGHS 330 POUNDS.**

(4.5 m)

(150 kg)

# THEODORE ROOSEVELT KEPT LOBSTERS AND A GIANT TORTOISE

IN HIS
**ROOM**
DURING
**COLLEGE.**

A SLUG HAS MORE TEETH THAN A SHARK.

Vietnamese mossy **frogs'** skin and eyes match the color of the **moss** in the caves that they live in.

Some freshwater **leeches** can live **10** months without **eating.**

In England's Victorian era, hedgehogs were kept to eat cockroaches and earwigs.

MALE OSTRICHES CAN ROAR!

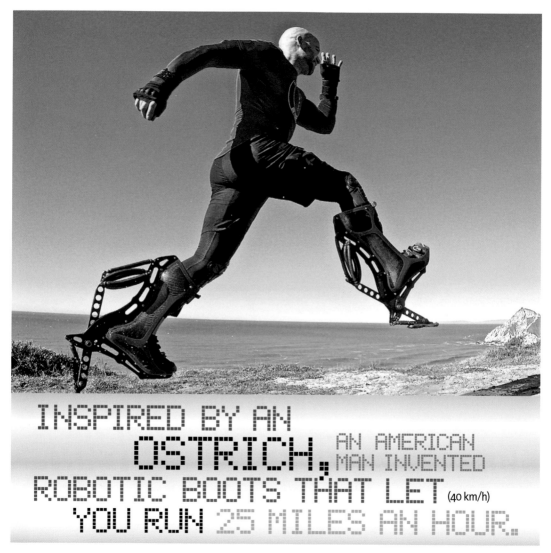

INSPIRED BY AN OSTRICH, AN AMERICAN MAN INVENTED ROBOTIC BOOTS THAT LET YOU RUN 25 MILES AN HOUR. (40 km/h)

**NEW GUINEA SINGING DOGS COMMUNICATE THROUGH TUNEFUL YODELS.**

AN EGYPTIAN FRUIT BAT'S LONG TONGUE STAYS COILED AROUND ITS RIB CAGE WHEN IT'S NOT EATING.

When male **chameleons** see their **reflection** in a **mirror, they change color**, thinking that the image **is a rival.**

A **hydra**— a small, freshwater creature— can open its **mouth wider** than its body.

PANDAS HAVE A TOUGH LINING IN THEIR THROAT THAT PROTECTS THEM FROM BAMBOO SPLINTERS.

**Scientists think that the giant panda's black-and-white colors help keep it hidden in both snow and dark forests.**

**A mythical two-tailed lion**  **is a state animal of Czechia.**

**SLUGS HAVE GREEN BLOOD.**

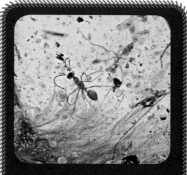

THE FEATHERED TAIL OF A **99-MILLION-YEAR-OLD DINOSAUR** WAS FOUND IN A **PIECE OF AMBER** SOLD AT A **MYANMAR MARKET.**

**CATS HAVE WHISKERS ON THEIR FRONT LEGS.**

**Pigcasso,** a 450-pound pig from South Africa, (204-kg) **paints on canvas** using a paintbrush that she holds in her mouth.

squeak!

A baby pigeon is called a squeaker.

The psychedelic **frogfish** uses its fins to *jump* off the seafloor, then shoots water out of its **gills** to move *forward*.

The Aztec name for armadillo translates as "turtle rabbit."

REGGAE AND SOFT ROCK
MUSIC CAN HELP DOGS RELAX.

FROM A SITTING POSITION, **CATS** CAN SPRING UP TO NINE TIMES THEIR HEIGHT.

# Rattlesnakes can inject only one-third of their venom when biting through denim.

# African jacana birds carry their chicks under their wing.

# A MOTHER SEA TURTLE'S HATCHLINGS ARE MORE LIKELY TO BE FEMALE IF THE SAND WHERE SHE BURIES HER EGGS IS WARM.

**Dally, a Jack Russell terrier, rides around on a miniature horse named Spanky.**

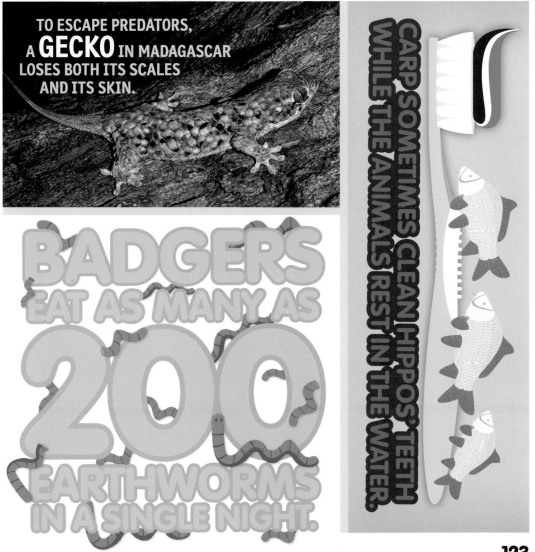

TO ESCAPE PREDATORS, A **GECKO** IN MADAGASCAR LOSES BOTH ITS SCALES AND ITS SKIN.

CARP SOMETIMES CLEAN HIPPOS' TEETH WHILE THE ANIMALS REST IN THE WATER.

BADGERS EAT AS MANY AS 200 EARTHWORMS IN A SINGLE NIGHT.

**Parrots will** give one another **high fives** with their **feet.**

*Schoolkids* in Kirkwall, Scotland, *gave their deceased* pet *goldfish* a Viking burial, setting Freddy and Bubbles afloat in a *flaming boat.*

Mosquitoes don't **usually bite** in temperatures **below 50°F.** (10°C)

A TOWN IN ALASKA, U.S.A., IS CALLED CHICKEN.

# Snow leopards can leap
# 30 feet (9 m)
## in one bound.

**A KING SALMON**

CAUGHT IN 1985 IN ALASKA, U.S.A.,

WEIGHED MORE THAN 97 POUNDS. (44 kg)

THE SALLY LIGHTFOOT CRAB GOT ITS NAME FROM BEING ABLE TO RUN *FORWARD*, BACKWARD, AND SIDE TO SIDE.

The **EAGLE** is the most **COMMON** TEAM NICKNAME in U.S. COLLEGE SPORTS.

WILD GREATER HONEYGUIDE **BIRDS** IN AFRICA TWEET AND FLUTTER IN FRONT OF HUMAN HONEY HUNTERS TO LEAD THEM TO **BEE-HIVES.**

George Washington **loved breeding mules.**

In UGANDA, **MONGOOSES** CLIMB ON **warthogs,** PICKING OFF AND **eating ticks.**

131

The screaming hairy armadillo got its name because it screams loudly when threatened.

ICELAND TRADITION SAYS THAT THE "YULE CAT" EATS ANYONE WHO DOESN'T RECEIVE NEW CLOTHES BEFORE CHRISTMAS.

**Pom-pom crabs** carry **sea anemones** in their **claws** and wave them around when threatened.

NEWBORN GIRAFFES CAN *RUN* AN HOUR AFTER THEY ARE BORN.

Domestic cows can see almost all around themselves without moving their heads.

THE CHANG BUILDING IN BANGKOK, THAILAND, IS SHAPED TO LOOK LIKE AN ELEPHANT.

There are some **40,000 species of snails and slugs.**

At a pop-up restaurant in London, England, **dogs dined** on foods including **seaweed** and **kale.**

# AT BIRTH, THE WHALE SHARK— THE BIGGEST FISH IN THE OCEAN— IS ABOUT THE LENGTH OF TWO PENCILS LINED UP END-TO-END.

Zoos and aquariums across the United States had a **Cute Animal Tweet-Off,** a battle for the best baby animal photo.

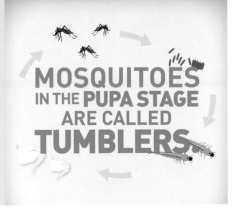

MOSQUITOES IN THE **PUPA STAGE** ARE CALLED **TUMBLERS.**

Abraham Lincoln's sons had their **pet goats** pull them chariot-style on kitchen chairs through the **White House.**

WHEN THREATENED, THE *MOCK VIPER* CAN CHANGE THE SHAPE OF ITS PUPILS TO SLITS TO LOOK LIKE A *DEADLY VIPER*.

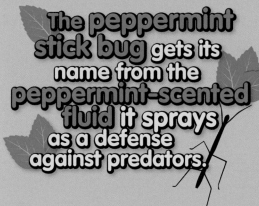

The **peppermint stick bug** gets its name from the peppermint-scented **fluid** it sprays as a defense against predators.

The **strawberry squid** has a **giant eye** that usually faces upward to gather light and a tiny one that looks below for prey.

141

The **caracal,** a small cat from Asia and Africa, can **leap** over a **nine-foot-tall fence.** (3-m)

One college's official **mascot** is the **banana slug.**

**DRILL MONKEYS GRIN** TO KEEP THINGS CALM WHEN THEY MEET OTHER MONKEYS.

RATS SHAKE THEIR HEADS WHEN GIVEN WATER THAT TASTES BAD.

# HAGFISH HAVE NO BONES.

**Wrinkle-faced bats pull up a mask made of their own skin to cover their faces while they sleep.**

Researchers are making **biodegradable plastic bags** out of **shrimp shells.**

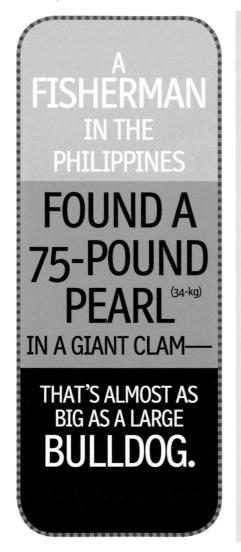

A FISHERMAN IN THE PHILIPPINES FOUND A 75-POUND PEARL (34-kg) IN A GIANT CLAM—

THAT'S ALMOST AS BIG AS A LARGE BULLDOG.

A woman in Virginia, U.S.A., found a yellow anaconda

in her apartment toilet.

AUSTRALIA'S **THORNY DEVIL LIZARD** "**DRINKS**" WATER BY ABSORBING MOISTURE FROM WET SAND THROUGH ITS SKIN.

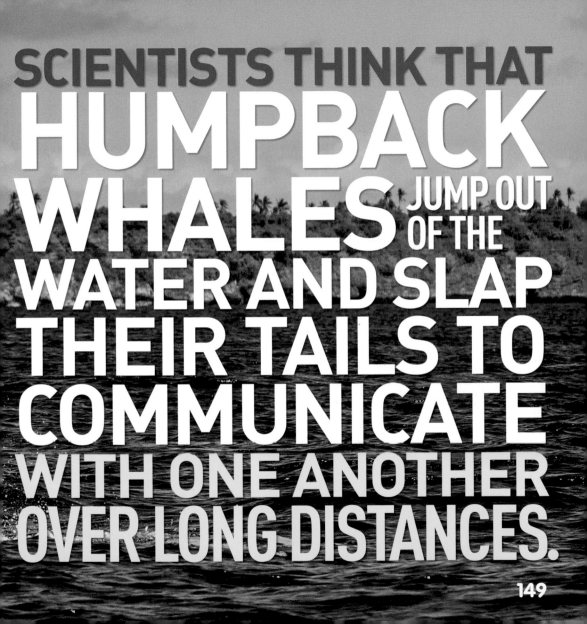

SCIENTISTS THINK THAT HUMPBACK WHALES JUMP OUT OF THE WATER AND SLAP THEIR TAILS TO COMMUNICATE WITH ONE ANOTHER OVER LONG DISTANCES.

A frog's tongue— 10 times softer than a human's— is the texture of brain tissue.

A BABY OYSTER IS CALLED A SPAT.

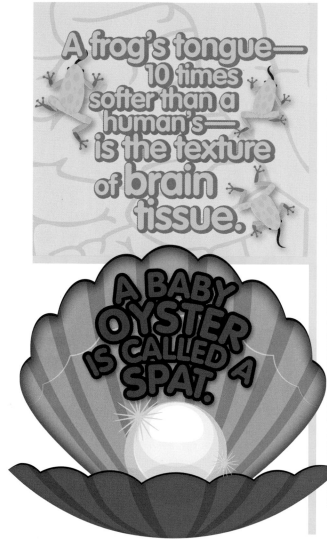

FOSSILIZED ANT IN AMBER

AN ANT SPECIES THAT LIVED ABOUT 100 MILLION YEARS AGO LOOKED LIKE MODERN PORTRAYALS OF ALIENS.

GOATS CAN HAVE DIFFERENT ACCENTS, JUST LIKE HUMANS DO.

**NATIONAL GOAT AWARENESS WEEK OCCURS EVERY JUNE.**

The paca, a rodent prized for its meat, is nicknamed the "royal rat" because it was served to **Queen Elizabeth II** on her 1985 visit to Belize.

THE **LUMPSUCKER FISH** HAS SUCTION CUPS ON ITS BELLY THAT ALLOW IT TO HOLD ON TO ALGAE IN THE OCEAN.

Some *pampered pooches* wear dog collars worth more than *three million dollars*

**Fish tails** move side to side, but **dolphin** and **whale tails** move up and down.

SOME **BOTTLENOSE DOLPHINS HERD FISH** INTO SHALLOW WATER AND **LAUNCH THEMSELVES** ONTO THE BEACH TO CATCH THEM.

**HUMMINGBIRDS CAN FLY UPSIDE DOWN.**

WHEN FOOD SUPPLIES ARE LOW, PIRANHAS WILL EAT EACH OTHER.

A rescued sloth in Suriname, South America, was potty-trained.

Millions of **bioluminescent firefly squid** surface in Japan's Toyama Bay from March to June every year, creating an **electric blue shoreline.**

Two **goat brothers** in Palm Beach, Florida, U.S.A., learned how to **paddleboard.**

The stomach juices of **vultures** can neutralize deadly diseases.

SOME
**TERMITES**
CAN BUILD
MOUNDS AS
TALL AS A
**THREE-
STORY
HOUSE.**

Four-eyed **frogs** from South America have only **two eyes;** the other two "eyes" are poisonous glands.

The world's population of **spiders** weighs as much as *500 Titanics*.

**CUVIER'S BEAKED WHALES** CAN DIVE DOWN TO NEARLY **10,000** (3,048 m) **FEET** AND STAY SUBMERGED FOR **TWO HOURS.**

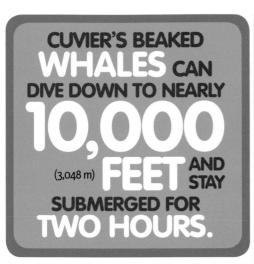

*You can buy perfume for your dog.*

TINY PADS IN THE **HOOVES** OF **KLIPSPRINGERS** ACT LIKE **SUCTION CUPS** TO HELP THEM **BALANCE** AS THEY HOP BETWEEN ROCKS.

The word "crocodile" in Greek means "worm of the stones."

**Beavers slap their tails on the water when they feel threatened.**

OUT OF A MILLION ATLANTIC MACKEREL FISH EGGS, ONLY 1 TO 10 SURVIVE.

**Antlers improve a male moose's hearing.**

**Pumpkin, a rescued raccoon that lives in the Bahamas, has over a million followers on social media.**

JAPANESE MACAQUES CAN SWIM THE EQUIVALENT OF 10 LAPS IN AN OLYMPIC-SIZE POOL.

SKIN THAT HELP THEM GLIDE THROUGH THE AIR.

**SNOWY TREE CRICKETS CHIRP IN SYNC.**

In the movie **The Princess Bride,** *the Rodent of Unusual Size was played by an actor in a* **rat suit.**

A giant **squid's brain** is shaped like a **doughnut.**

**EACH TIME A RATTLESNAKE SHEDS ITS SKIN, IT ADDS A NEW SEGMENT TO ITS RATTLE.**

The tundra swan has the most feathers of any bird— about 25,000.

An Ohio, U.S.A., company is developing **sports helmets** inspired by hedgehog spines, which help protect the animal when it falls.

OCTOPUS **INK** CAN TEMPORARILY **BLIND** PREDATORS.

SOME **VEINED OCTOPUSES** WALK ALONG THE SEAFLOOR CARRYING

# Octopuses can change the texture of their skin to blend in with bumpy coral and rocks.

A COCONUT SHELL TO HIDE UNDER IF THEY NEED PROTECTION.

**RED PANDAS** USE SCENT GLANDS IN THEIR FOOTPADS TO MARK THEIR TERRITORY.

The word **"ferret"** means **"little thief."**

The Asian grass **lizard's tail** is more than three times the length of its body.

**U.S. PRESIDENT** HERBERT HOOVER HAD A **DOG** NAMED **KING TUT.**

THE LAUGHING KOOKABURRA BIRD SOUNDS LIKE A MONKEY.

Some honeybees beat their wings more than 200 times a minute.

A SLOTH BEAR'S **NOSTRILS** CAN CLOSE COMPLETELY TO PROTECT ITS **NOSE** FROM DUST AND INSECTS.

**SLOTH BEARS** HAVE FLOPPY, LOOSE LIPS THAT ALLOW THEM TO **SLURP UP INSECTS** EASILY.

The **arctic fox** is the only land **mammal** native to Iceland.

THE U.S. **NATIONAL ZOO** IN WASHINGTON, D.C., GAVE **BAO BAO,** A THREE-YEAR-OLD **GIANT PANDA,** A CAKE MADE OF ICE, BAMBOO, APPLE JUICE, AND BISCUITS.

KiWi BIRDS' BILLS CAN DETECT VIBRATIONS FROM WORMS IN THE SOIL.

A human and a cat were buried together 9,500 years ago on the Mediterranean island of Cyprus.

The northern clingfish has a suction cup on its belly that is so strong it can rip mollusks 150 times its weight off the seafloor.

ALL TURTLES LACK TEETH.

BABY SEAHORSES CAN **EAT** ABOUT **3,000 PIECES** OF FOOD A DAY.

SEAHORSES DON'T HAVE STOMACHS— OR TEETH.

**SEAHORSE COUPLES** SOMETIMES **HOLD TAILS** WHEN TRAVELING THROUGH **SEAGRASS.**

An **adult walrus** can eat as many as **6,000 clams** in one meal.

WALRUSES WILL **ADOPT** ABANDONED PUPS.

WALRUSES HAVE AIR POCKETS IN THEIR THROATS

TO HELP THEM STAY AFLOAT WHEN THEY SLEEP.

# SOME TYPES OF BATS MAKE ULTRASONIC CALLS THROUGH THEIR NOSTRILS INSTEAD OF THROUGH THEIR MOUTH.

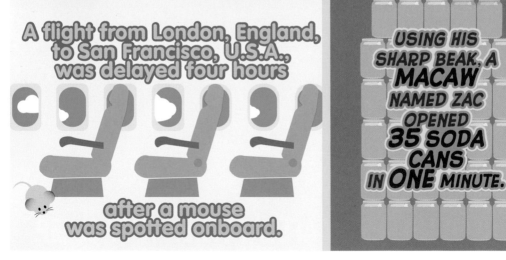

A flight from London, England, to San Francisco, U.S.A., was delayed four hours after a mouse was spotted onboard.

USING HIS SHARP BEAK, A **MACAW** NAMED ZAC OPENED **35 SODA CANS** IN **ONE** MINUTE.

IN THE EARLY 20TH CENTURY, **400 MILLION** BLACK-TAILED PRAIRIE DOGS LIVED **IN A SINGLE COLONY** IN TEXAS, U.S.A.

**Gunnison's prairie dogs** will use different alarm calls depending on the type of predator.

THE WATERS OFF THE GALÁPAGOS ISLANDS ARE HOME TO THE DENSEST SHARK POPULATION IN THE WORLD—34 TONS OF SHARKS PER ACRE.

(31 t)

(0.4 ha)

**VELVET WORMS SQUIRT THEIR PREY WITH A STICKY, QUICK-HARDENING SLIME.**

Male kangaroos are sometimes called boomers.

Some **black bears** living in British Columbia, Canada, are born with white fur.

THE NOISE A **PIG** MAKES IN ENGLISH IS OINK; IT'S BOO-BO IN JAPANESE; AND IT'S CHRUM CHRUM IN POLISH.

THE NOISE A **BEE** MAKES IN ENGLISH IS BUZZ;

IT'S BOONG-BOONG IN KOREAN; AND IN GERMAN IT'S SUMMEN.

THE NOISE A FROG MAKES IN ENGLISH IS RIBBIT;

IN ITALIAN IT'S CRA CRA; AND IN HUNGARIAN IT'S BRE-KE-KE.

# FACTFINDER

**Boldface** indicates illustrations.

# FACTFINDER

# FACTFINDER

Since 1888, the National Geographic Society has funded more than 12,000 research, exploration, and preservation projects around the world. The Society receives funds from National Geographic Partners, LLC, funded in part by your purchase. A portion of the proceeds from this book supports this vital work. To learn more, visit natgeo.com/info.

For more information, visit nationalgeographic .com, call 1-800-647-5463, or write to the following address:

National Geographic Partners
1145 17th Street N.W.
Washington, D.C. 20036-4688 U.S.A.

Visit us online at
nationalgeographic.com/books

For librarians and teachers:
ngchildrensbooks.org

More for kids from National Geographic:
natgeokids.com

For information about special discounts for bulk purchases, please contact National Geographic Books Special Sales: specialsales@natgeo.com

For rights or permissions inquiries, please contact National Geographic Books Subsidiary Rights: bookrights@natgeo.com

Designed by Rachael Hamm Plett of Moduza Design

Trade paperback ISBN: 978-1-4263-2981-4
Reinforced library binding ISBN: 978-1-4263-2982-1

Printed in China
17/PPS/1

The publisher would like to thank Grace Smith, project manager; Julie Beer, researcher and author; Michelle Harris, researcher and author; Hillary Leo, photo editor; Paige Towler, project editor; Lori Epstein, photo director; Molly Reid, production editor; and Anne LeongSon and Gus Tello, design production assistants.

## PHOTO CREDITS

# Beyond WEIRD!

NATIONAL GEOGRAPHIC KiDS

ANIMAL RECORDS

THE BIGGEST, *FASTEST*, GROSSEST, TINIEST, SLOWEST, AND SMELLIEST CREATURES ON THE PLANET

KATHY FURGANG AND SARAH WASSNER FLYNN

STRONGEST

DEADLIEST

BIGGEST

TINIEST

Discover which creatures RULE the animal kingdom in all kinds of cool categories—fastest, tiniest, smartest, smelliest, deadliest, and more!

MOST POISONOUS